POSONIUM. PRESBURG

BRATISLAVA

100 Photos & Engravings
History & Sights
Surroundings
Map of city centre

MARTIN SLOBODA

PAST AND PRESENT

Whether you are planning a visit to this city on the Danube, or whether you best way to get acquainted with the city when you first arrive is to take a stroll through its cobbled streets. In the historic Old Town you can follow in the footsteps of famous composers,

View of the Old Town and the Castle looking west.

have already found your way here, you will soon discover that Bratislava, Slovakia's colourful capital, has a great deal to offer. Perhaps the

Bratislava has a rich musical tradition. In summer, the streets of the town are transformed into musical venues.

venerable archbishops and even noble kings. Dozens of palaces, churches and the mighty Castle still bear witness today to the impressive spiritual and worldly power of the former rulers. Bratislava (population 430,000) is situated in the south-western corner of the country, practically on the borders of two other states – Austria and Hungary. After the split of Czechoslovakia in 1993, the city became the seat of the Slovak parliament, government and president. It is not just the political but also the economic, cultural and scientific centre of the country. Bratislava is also the seat of three universities with a total

HISTORICAL OVERVIEW

100 BC Biatec
Celtic oppidum

864 Dowina
First written record of Devín Castle in the annals of Fulda

907 Brezalauspurch
First written record of the town in the annals of Salzburg

AD 300-400
Roman station Gerulata in today's Rusovce

One of the most beautiful views of the Castle is from a boat or from the opposite bank of the Danube.

coming one of the most dynamic in Europe. Lying just 60km downstream from Vienna, these are the closest neighbours of all the world's capitals and, due to the fact that there was an electric train connection even before the First World War, Bratislava used to be called "a suburb of Vienna". But there is far more connecting the two cities than a train and a common history and cultural heritage. Thanks to recent reconstruction efforts, the Slovak capital is shining again in its original splendour, while, just like Vienna, it has retained a nostalgic atmosphere from bygone days.

of 60,000 students, who form part and parcel of the lively atmosphere of the Old Town streets and squares.

Thanks to its strategic location, its excellent infrastructure and highly educated population, Bratislava is now a magnet for inward investment, helping the Slovak economy grow at an unprecedented rate. As the largest city in the country, Bratislava accounts for 26 per cent of Slovakia's GDP and is the engine driving the country. It is already apparent that the surrounding region is rapidly be-

Michalská ulica (St. Michael's Street) abounds with cafés, shops and galleries.

1241 - 1242
Invasion and devastation by hordes of Tatars

1436
King Sigismund of Luxembourg grants the town its coat-of-arms

1465 King Matthias Corvinus founds Universitas Istropolitana - the first university within the territory of present-day Slovakia

Around 1000
Stephen I, founder of the kingdom of Hungary

1291
Andrew III grants the town municipal privileges

1526
After the Battle of Mohacs, large parts of Hungary fall under Ottoman rule

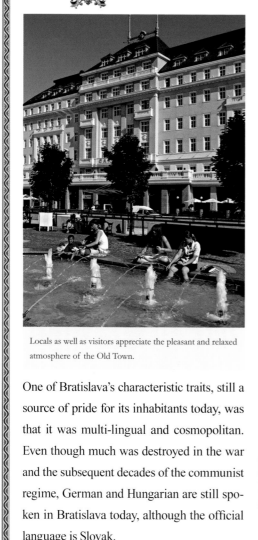

Locals as well as visitors appreciate the pleasant and relaxed atmosphere of the Old Town.

While Bratislava cannot compete in size with nearby Vienna and Budapest, locals and foreign visitors alike appreciate it for its charming narrow little streets, friendly courtyards and many other attractions found in the pleasant and compact historical centre, which is traffic-free. Opera performances, concerts, numerous museums and galleries - from classical to contemporary - are part of the enriching experience to be had in this city renowned for its varied cultural life.

Discover the charming Old Town with its traditional cafés, cosy courtyards and old wine cellars and feel welcome in the city's many hotels and restaurants. Bratislava and its surroundings, boasting castles, chateaux and a wine-growing

Tradition and nostalgia make the Old Town a delightful place.

One of Bratislava's characteristic traits, still a source of pride for its inhabitants today, was that it was multi-lingual and cosmopolitan. Even though much was destroyed in the war and the subsequent decades of the communist regime, German and Hungarian are still spoken in Bratislava today, although the official language is Slovak.

HISTORICAL OVERVIEW

1536 - 1783
Pressburg serves as the capital of Hungary

1552 - 1783
Hungarian Crown Jewels guarded in the Castle's Crown Tower

1563 - 1830
Pressburg serves as the coronation town of Hungary

17
Coronation of Maria There in St Martin's Cathed

In summer, the streets and squares of Bratislava bustle with life far into the night.

region with the country's finest wines, deserve more than a half-day's stopover on your tour of Central Europe.

We hope that what you discover in these pages will be enough to convince you that your stay will be a rewarding experience and this guidebook will help you make the most of your time here.

Nature, art and the peculiar passion of sovereigns provided the free royal capital and coronation town Pressburg with such diverse assets that just like other strange towns it deserves a proper description.

Johann Matthias Korabinsky 1781

5

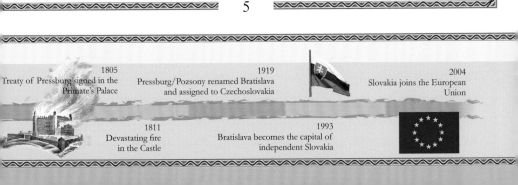

1805
Treaty of Pressburg signed in the Primate's Palace

1811
Devastating fire in the Castle

1919
Pressburg/Pozsony renamed Bratislava and assigned to Czechoslovakia

1993
Bratislava becomes the capital of independent Slovakia

2004
Slovakia joins the European Union

RICH HISTORY

Archaeological evidence suggests prehistoric habitation of the area of Bratislava, which attracted ancient peoples whose settlements date back to the Stone Age. Among the earliest known settlers are the Celts whose settlement - Oppidum - on the Castle Hill, dating from as early as the first century BC, is considered to be one of the centres of their civilisation along the Danube.

Numerous coins showing the Celtic prince Biatec (first century BC) have been found in the city.

Nor could the Romans afford to ignore the

Relief carving from the excavated Roman military station Gerulata in present-day Rusovce, to the south of Bratislava.

strategic position of this site stretching between the Danube and the slopes of the Little Carpathians - they established themselves on the river's north bank in order to defend the Danube that marked the limit of their empire against the attacks of 'barbarian' clans from the north. Bricks with stamps of the XIV Legion found in the city are evidence of their presence.

The country experienced a difficult period after the fall of the mighty Roman Empire and the withdrawal of its legions due to invasions by tribes from the east. The overall migration brought Germanic tribes to the region and, from the 7th century onwards, the Slavs, who later established the Great Moravian Empire. Their fortresses Dowina (Devín Castle) and Brezalauspurch (Bratislava) were first referred to in the annals of Fulda (864) and Salzburg (907). Brezalauspurch is assumed to derive from the name of a Slavic prince and, as well as being a fortified settlement, it also contained a large Christian church with a cemetery. Coins have been found dating from the 11th century bearing the inscription Preslava or Breslava. There is further evidence that in the 12th century the name Bresburg was widely used - hence the German form Pressburg. There are others from the same period, too. Posonium, the Latin form of the name, stems from the 12th century's Possen or Bosonium and it later gave rise to the Hungarian version Pozsony. Whatever the name, however, they are all of Slavic origin. Thus in 1919, when the city was officially renamed Bratislava from Pressburg (German) and Pozsony (Hungarian), it regained a form close to its original.

After the Great Moravian Empire had been defeated by Magyar (Hungarian) tribes, the new rulers took possession of the country as far as the Morava River to the west of the city. Stephen I, who became their first king and was later canonised, invited new settlers mainly from German-speaking countries. The 11th century saw Bratislava strength-

Emperor Heinrich III during his siege of Pressburg in 1052. One of the enemy soldiers tries to sink the Emperor's boats on the Danube. Vienna Chronicle (1358).

Exhibitions of the Archaeological Museum in the Castle display real treasures dating from the Stone Age to the Middle Ages.

ening its position as a frontier fortress of Hungary and was thus twice besieged by Emperor Heinrich III in 1042 and 1052, although the second time was without success.

King Bela III in the 12th century was determined to establish diplomatic relations with Western Europe and after the Pope demanded that Hungary contribute troops to the Third Crusade to the Holy Land, thorough preparations were started. This is documented in King Bela III's correspondence with the English King Henry II in 1188. The following year Emperor Friedrich I Barbarossa left Regensburg with his troops for Pressburg in order to join the Hungarians and confer on the basic strategies of the crusade. Legend has it that in 1211 King András (Andrew) II engaged his daughter Elisabeth to Landgrave Ludwig IV of Thuringia (Thüringen) at Pressburg Castle. Following the engagement, the four-year-old Elisabeth was taken to Wartburg Castle

Pressburg on the edge of a map of Vienna (1438-1455).

(Thuringia,Germany) where she married in 1221. After her husband's death she devoted her life to charity, helping the poor and the sick, for which she was canonised in 1235. In 1241 hordes of Mongol fighters from Asia invaded the country from the east and their ravages extended as far as Pressburg. They were, however, unable to capture the town and it was thus one of the few towns in the country to withstand their attacks. A greater disaster came in 1271 when King Otakar II of Bohemia besieged and subsequently took the town.

The year 1291 saw the town being granted extensive privileges by King András III, leading to an increase in the town's population and wealth.

Sigismund of Luxembourg ascended the Hungarian throne in the 15th century and had the Castle rebuilt at great expense as his residence in Hungary. In fear of the Hussites, who had already devastated much of the country, the town determined to strengthen its fortifications in 1427. The Hussite leaders finally came to the town in 1429 to negotiate with the King in the present-day Old Town Hall. King Sigismund of Luxembourg renewed all the municipal privileges and in 1436 granted the town its coat-of-arms, which has been used ever since. By the 15th century, Pressburg was a flourishing centre of culture and commerce, the major trade commodity being wine, which by the 16th century was being exported all over Europe. During the reign of King Matthias Corvinus,

The two oldest churches in the Old Town. From the left: Franciscan Church (13th century), Church of the Poor Clares (14th century).

Pressburg enjoyed a period of prosperity and thrived at a high cultural level. In 1465 the Renaissance ruler founded the Universitas Istropolitana here, the first university

By this royal charter(1436), King Sigismund of Luxembourg renewed all municipal privileges and granted the town its coat-of-arms, which has been used ever since.

nation took place in St Martin's Cathedral. Pressburg retained its position as the political and cultural centre of Hungary until the late 18th century.

The 17th century brought difficult times to the whole country. A devastating civil war, the Turkish occupation, incompetent statesmen and the continual state of warfare brought in overall misery and hampered any progress. Pressburg was not spared either. The religious freedom that its citizens had hitherto enjoyed was repressed with the arrival of the imperial troops in 1672, whereupon the Protestants lost their schools and churches.

within the territory of present-day Slovakia, which counted scholars of European fame among its professors. Thanks to his second wife, Beatrice of Naples, Matthias Corvinus looked to Italy and became a patron of the arts who aimed at creating a similar Renaissance environment in Hungary.

Following the disastrous Battle of Mohács in 1526, in which King Louis II and many nobles were killed and the Hungarians defeated, the Turks took control of two-thirds of the country, including the capital Buda. In 1536, the Hungarian Diet declared Pressburg to be the capital of the kingdom and after that, as the centre of the kingdom, it enjoyed rapid development and grew wealthier. The government, the viceroy, the nobility, the Diet and the Archbishop - all moved to the town and finally in 1563 the first coro-

Illustration of a battle against Turks.

The reign of Maria Theresa, Queen of Hungary (1740-1780), was a golden age for Pressburg, both culturally and socially. Thanks to the Queen's presence, the town experienced unprecedented development, which resulted in the conversion of the Castle into her

Pressburg from the south. Coloured engraving by Hogenberg, 16th century.

sumptuous residence and the establishment of the Hungarian noble guard. Right up to the end of her days, Maria Theresa retained a special affection for Pressburg, where she frequently held court. The then cultural and commercial boom is also attributed to the residence of her son-in-law, Duke Albert of Sachsen-Teschen, Viceroy of Hungary, and Maria Theresa's favourite daughter, Maria Christine, both of whom took up residence in a new palace attached to the Castle.

The reign of Maria Theresa's reformist successor, Joseph II, brought an end to the town's heyday by transferring the capital to Buda (Budapest) in 1783.

The Napoleonic wars during the reign of Francis I brought universal suffering and Pressburg did not escape this either. On 26 December 1805, however, the Hall of Mirrors of the town's Primate's Palace became the venue for the signing of the Treaty of Pressburg following the Battle of the Three Emperors at Austerlitz (today Slavkov in the

The natural setting of the town of Pressburg is in an appealing and pleasant area, generously providing its inhabitants with all necessary means of keep.

Johann Matthias Korabinsky 1781

Czech Republic). In 1809, French troops led by Marshal Davout again besieged Pressburg from the opposite bank of the Danube and finally managed to capture it.

In 1741 Queen Maria Theresa came to the session of the Hungarian Diet in the Castle to ask in her famous speech for the support of the Hungarian aristocracy. Before she came to the end of her speech, the nobles had raised their swords and cried: "Vitam et sanguinem pro regina nostra!".

Despite the transfer of Hungary's capital to Buda, Pressburg re-established its importance in the second half of the 19th century - this time, however, as a rapidly expanding industrial centre. Traditionally, more German was spoken than Hungarian - and before 1918 very little Slovak - in what is today a meeting point of three countries.

Only at the beginning of the 20th century did Hungarian become on a par with German. Most inhabitants, however, communicated in both languages and, with the addition of Slovak after World War I, the city became truly tri-lingual. After the war and the break-up of the Austro-Hungarian empire, the city was assigned to the newly established Czechoslovak Republic in 1919 as an important port on the Danube and officially renamed Bratislava. During World War II, Bratislava served as

Napoleon besieged the town twice – in 1805 and 1809.

the capital of the Slovak fascist puppet state and it was only the national uprising in 1944 that saved the country from being counted among the losers of the war. Following the war, Czechoslovakia was restored, but a subsequent coup d'etat brought communism to power.

It was only in 1989 that the Velvet Revolution brought an end to it. 1993 saw the Velvet Divorce of the union into the independent Czech and Slovak Republics with Bratislava becoming the capital of the latter. Thanks to a high level of education,the low average

A popular electric train connected Vienna and Bratislava from 1914.

age,a strong economic background and an excellent location, Bratislava is perceived as one of the regions of Europe with the greatest growth potential.

Today, the Grassalkovich Palace serves as the residence of the President.

THE CASTLE ❶

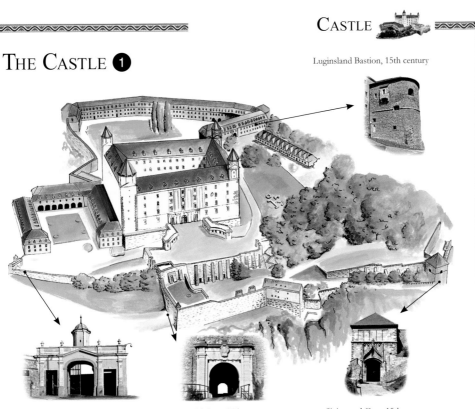

Luginsland Bastion, 15th century

Vienna Gate, 18th century   Leopold Gate, 17th century   Sigismund Gate, 15th century

One of the city's landmarks which, due to its silhouette, the locals quite appropriately call an "upturned table", was formerly a frontier stronghold and later the residence of the Hungarian kings. Towering on the Castle Hill 85 metres above the Danube, standing guardian over the Old Town, the Castle saw its golden age in the eighteenth century during the reign of Maria Theresa of Austria, who frequently held court here as Queen of Hungary. After the Celts and later the Romans, each of whom occupied the hill, the Slavs recognised its strategic position and in the ninth century built a fortified settlement with a large Christian church, the foundations of which are visible on the eastern terrace. The Castle is first mentioned in the annals of Salzburg in AD 907 in connection with the loss of the Bavarian army against Magyar (Hungarian) troops near "Brezalauspurch". The older Slavic fort was taken over by the Hungarians after their conquest of the Great Moravian Empire and incorporated in the eleventh century into the frontier defence system of the young Kingdom of Hungary. The thirteenth century saw extensive building activity on the Castle. A mighty new Romanesque tower with several defence towers was built.

The Castle acquired its present appearance in the fifteenth century, after King Sigismund

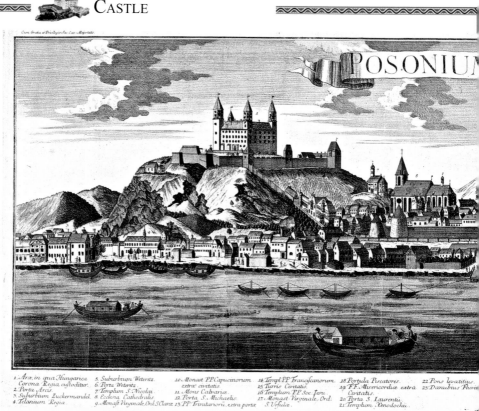

Cum Gratia et Privilegio Sac. Cæs. Majestatis

POSONIUM

1. Arx in qua Hungarica
   Corona Regia custoditur.
2. Porta Arcis.
3. Suburbium Zuckermandel.
4. Telonaum Regia.
5. Suburbium Wetertz.
6. Porta Weterz.
7. Templum S. Nicolai.
8. Ecclesia Cathedralis.
9. Monast. Virginale, Ord. S. Clare.
10. Monast PP Capucinorum extra civitatis.
11. Mons Calvariæ.
12. Porta S. Michaelis.
13. PP Trinitariorii extra portæ S. Michælis.
14. Templ PP Francscanorum.
15. Turris Civitatis.
16. Templum PP Soc. Jesu.
17. Monast Virginale, Ord. S. Ursulæ.
18. Portula Piscatores.
19. FF. Misericordiæ extra Civitatis.
20. Porta S. Laurentii.
21. Templum Xenodochii.
22. Pons levatitius.
23. Danubius Fluvi

Panoramic view of Pressburg from the south. Coloured engraving by Propst - Werner, c 1760.

of Luxembourg chose it as his residence in Hungary. The Tower was demol;ished and instead a large four-wing Gothic palace was erected, incorporating one of the defence towers. The system of defences was extended and from the east a new richly decorated entrance gate - the Sigismund Gate - was added. The outer wall of the Palace's west wing - since it needed to function as a defensive wall at the same time - is an incredible 11 metres thick. The well under the courtyard dates back to the fifteenth century and with its depth of 85 metres reaches the level of the Danube. Until the eighteenth century the well was the only water supply for the Castle's inhabitants. Having defeated the Hungarians at the Battle

The statue of St Elisabeth, daughter of the Hungarian King Andrew II, who was engaged in the Castle in 1211. Following her husband's death, she devoted her life to charity, for which she was later canonised.

of Mohács in 1526, the Turkish Ottoman Empire took control of extensive areas of Hungary. The royalty escaped from the capital

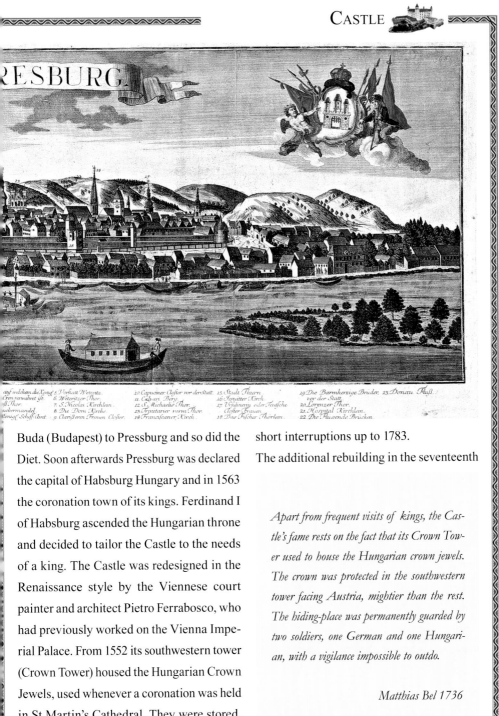

Buda (Budapest) to Pressburg and so did the Diet. Soon afterwards Pressburg was declared the capital of Habsburg Hungary and in 1563 the coronation town of its kings. Ferdinand I of Habsburg ascended the Hungarian throne and decided to tailor the Castle to the needs of a king. The Castle was redesigned in the Renaissance style by the Viennese court painter and architect Pietro Ferrabosco, who had previously worked on the Vienna Imperial Palace. From 1552 its southwestern tower (Crown Tower) housed the Hungarian Crown Jewels, used whenever a coronation was held in St Martin's Cathedral. They were stored, under close guard, in the Crown Tower with

short interruptions up to 1783.

The additional rebuilding in the seventeenth

Apart from frequent visits of kings, the Castle's fame rests on the fact that its Crown Tower used to house the Hungarian crown jewels. The crown was protected in the southwestern tower facing Austria, mightier than the rest. The hiding-place was permanently guarded by two soldiers, one German and one Hungarian, with a vigilance impossible to outdo.

Matthias Bel 1736

15

An aerial view of the Castle.

century saw the final storey and the remaining corner towers added, and the defensive system against Turkish attacks modernised. Essentially, it was these alterations that gave the Castle its present aspect.

Entrance gate to the cour d'honneur in front of the Castle proper.

The final remodelling - into a sumptuous Baroque residence - took place in the eighteenth century during the reign of Maria Theresa. As Queen of Hungary she promised the Hungarian nobility that she would spend more time in the country. This was the main reason for the extensive rebuilding of the Castle in order to meet the needs of the Queen. The interiors underwent a refurbishment in the Rococo style and from the outside a number of smaller annexes were attached to the main Palace. On the northern terrace, new French-style gardens were laid out and a new palace was added to the eastern wall, designed by Franz Anton Hillebrandt for Duke Albert von

In 1811 a devastating fire turned the Castle into rubble. Watercolour on engraving, 19th century.

After the devastating fire the Castle remained in ruins for the next 150 years.

Sachsen-Teschen, Viceroy of Hungary, and his wife Maria Christine, Maria Theresa's favourite daughter. It was here that the Duke finally found enough space for his extensive art collection. The town welcomed such high-ranking inhabitants, their presence attracting many of the nobility, who in turn drew famous composers to Pressburg which, thanks to them, flourished.

This golden age, however, was not to last long as Emperor Joseph II, Maria Theresa's successor and a great reformer, had the central offices transferred back to Buda (Budapest) in 1783 and the Duke left the Castle. His world-renowned art collection, having been

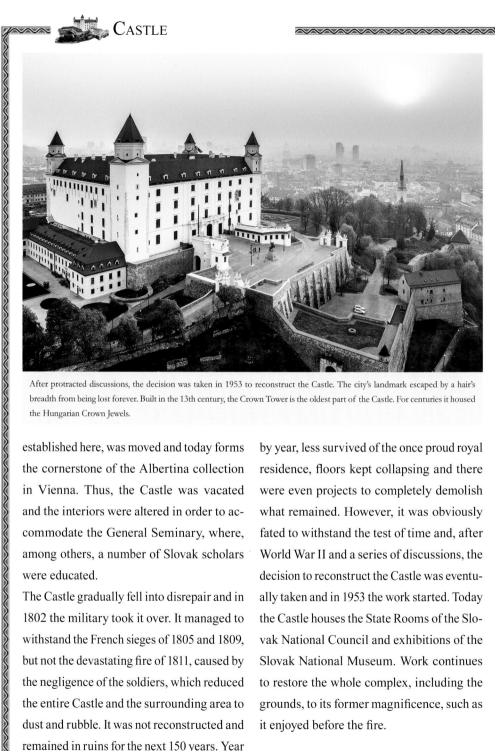

After protracted discussions, the decision was taken in 1953 to reconstruct the Castle. The city's landmark escaped by a hair's breadth from being lost forever. Built in the 13th century, the Crown Tower is the oldest part of the Castle. For centuries it housed the Hungarian Crown Jewels.

established here, was moved and today forms the cornerstone of the Albertina collection in Vienna. Thus, the Castle was vacated and the interiors were altered in order to accommodate the General Seminary, where, among others, a number of Slovak scholars were educated.

The Castle gradually fell into disrepair and in 1802 the military took it over. It managed to withstand the French sieges of 1805 and 1809, but not the devastating fire of 1811, caused by the negligence of the soldiers, which reduced the entire Castle and the surrounding area to dust and rubble. It was not reconstructed and remained in ruins for the next 150 years. Year by year, less survived of the once proud royal residence, floors kept collapsing and there were even projects to completely demolish what remained. However, it was obviously fated to withstand the test of time and, after World War II and a series of discussions, the decision to reconstruct the Castle was eventually taken and in 1953 the work started. Today the Castle houses the State Rooms of the Slovak National Council and exhibitions of the Slovak National Museum. Work continues to restore the whole complex, including the grounds, to its former magnificence, such as it enjoyed before the fire.

ST MARTIN'S CATHEDRAL ❷

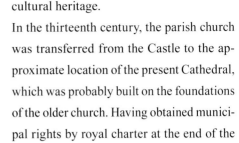

Presiding proudly over the western edge of the Old Town below the Castle Hill, St Martin's Cathedral witnessed between 1563-1830 a total of nineteen royal coronations. The former university and later coro-

St. Martin's Cathedral is one of Bratislava's landmarks. View from the Castle.

nation church surmounted by a model of St Stephen's crown towering 85 metres above the Old Town and commemorating its royal connection is one of the jewels of Slovakia's cultural heritage.

In the thirteenth century, the parish church was transferred from the Castle to the approximate location of the present Cathedral, which was probably built on the foundations of the older church. Having obtained municipal rights by royal charter at the end of the thirteenth century, the settlement below the Castle experienced rapid development and a growth in population.

Being too small for the town, the former church in the Romanesque style had to give way to a larger one and in the early fourteenth century work was begun on a new Gothic building inspired by hall churches in Swabia (Germany). The construction of the church continued into the fifteenth century and came under the direct influence of master masons at St Stephen's Cathedral in Vienna. Consecrated in 1452, its choir was subsequently demolished and replaced by a larger and more impressive one. Lavishly furnished in the Gothic period, the interior contained at least 27 altars, which were, however, not destined to survive the Baroque refurbishment.

This was initiated by a patron of the arts,

St Martin's Cathedral towering 85m above the Old Town.

Emmerich Eszterházy, Archbishop of Esztergom, in 1725. It was he who ordered the building of St John Elemosynarius Chapel (1729-1732), an extensive Baroque refurbishment of the choir, and a partial refurbishment of the nave and aisles. The Archbishop assigned the work to outstanding artists. He invited Georg Raphael Donner, a famous sculptor to the Austrian court, to come from Salzburg and establish his workshop in the summer residence of the Archbishop. During his eleven years in Pressburg he created the majority of his masterpieces. Donner designed the new High Altar with a monumental equestrian group of St Martin and the Beggar as its centrepiece. It is questionable whether the St John Elemosynarius Chapel was created by Donner or by another famous Austrian,

The 300kg gilded model of St Stephen's crown dating from 1765 tops the spire of St Martin's Cathedral and is an allusion to the period from 1563 to 1830 when Hungarian monarchs were crowned here.

St Martin's Cathedral. Nave looking east, c 1450.

In the past the western façade of St Martin's Cathedral was part of the town's fortification. Engraving by Engelbrecht, c 1735.

Fischer von Erlach. The elaborate sculptural decoration of the chapel and the altar with a silver shrine containing the body of St John Elemosynarius, the Alexandrian patriarch, as well as the memorial of the Archbishop are, however, the work of Donner.

The purist Neo-Gothic restoration in the nineteenth century caused nearly all elements of the intricate Baroque furnishing to be dismantled. After 1865 it was only the St John Elemosynarius Chapel at the eastern end of the north aisle and the centrepiece of the former High Altar - the equestrian statue in lead of St Martin and the Beggar - at the eastern end of the south aisle - that survived in their original form.

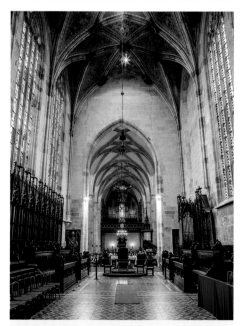

View of the presbytery built around 1470.

Maria Ludovica's coronation in St Martin's Cathedral in 1808. In the background the former High Altar with the statue of St Martin and the Beggar by Donner. Coloured engraving, 19th century.

Equestrian statue of St Martin and the Beggar by Raphael Donner (1733-1735) in the southeast corner of the nave. Formerly the centrepiece of the High Altar by the same artist.

St Martin's Cathedral was closely connected to the city's rich musical life in the past as well as now. The Church Music Society of St Martin, established in 1828, was able to organise many concerts of the works of famous composers. In 1834 Mozart's Requiem and a year later Beethoven's Missa Solemnis were performed here. As early as in 1840 Franz Liszt conducted the local orchestra here, later became a member of the Society and was a frequent visitor to Pressburg. In 1884 he conducted his own Coronation Mass in St Martin's Cathedral.

CORONATIONS

s the Turks had captured the ancient coronation town of the Hungarian kings - Székesfehérvár (50 km southeast of Budapest) and the seat of the Archbishop - Esztergom, it was decided that Pressburg should become the country's capital, the coronation town of the Hungarian kings as well as the seat of the Archbishop. Coronations took place in St Martin's Cathedral from 1563 and it was not until 1830 that the last ceremony took place in Pressburg before the coronation town was transferred to Budapest. Eleven sovereigns and eight of their royal spouses were anointed with holy oil, then crowned with St Stephen's crown in St Martin's Cathedral. All the sovereigns crowned in Pressburg were members of the

Maria Theresa as Hungarian Queen in Pressburg. Coloured engraving, 18th century.

Habsburg family.

Every coronation was preceded by a session of the Hungarian Diet, where those assembled gave their views on the election of a new sovereign. The Sovereign, the nobility and

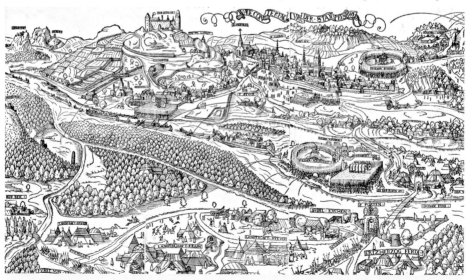

Description of Maximilian II's coronation in 1563 - the first to have taken place in Pressburg. Woodcut by Mayer, 1563.

After the actual coronation there followed theatrical spectacles, naval battles, knights' tournaments and folk amusements. After the coronation, the Sovereign paraded along the decorated streets, passing the Main Square towards the Franciscan Church, where he or she knighted selected nobles as Knights of the Golden Spur. From there, mounted on horseback, the Sovereign made his or her way through St Michael's Gate towards a large open space outside the town walls, where he or she took the oath. The last part of the route took the Sovereign to the Danube, where he or she mounted a little hill on horseback, which had been constructed from soil representing all parts of the country and brandished the sword in all directions, being prepared to fight anyone challenging the throne and to

A painting on the north wall of the choir shows a list of all the Hungarian monarchs crowned in St Martin's Cathedral.

not least the town spared no expense on the coronation ceremony and the subsequent procession and made it a magnificent pageant.

King Leopold II on the Coronation Hill near the Danube making his vow to protect the realm. Coloured engraving, 1790.

Every year there is a re-enactment of a different one of the 19 original coronations.

protect the realm. That concluded the official part of the ceremony and a coronation banquet followed. The tradition of coronation ceremonies comes alive annually on the last Saturday in June. The town's largest event attracts thousands of locals as well as visitors, who become part of a great procession accompanied with feasts, tournaments and the roasting of oxen.

The small brass crowns in the cobblestones mark the original route of the coronation procession. With the help of the map below, you can follow in the footsteps of the crowned monarchs through the Old Town's streets and squares.

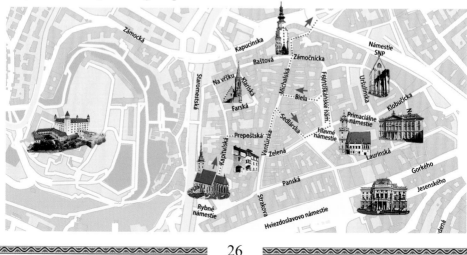

THE OLD TOWN HALL ❸

Lying directly at the heart of the Old Town, in Hlavné námestie (Main Square), the Old Town Hall with its tower is one of the landmarks of the Old Town. Over a period of five hundred years, decisions were taken in this building affecting the everyday life of the town. It was here that, under the presidency of the Mayor, sessions of the town council were held, court hearings took place and the town's leaders received important visitors, occasionally even kings.

The building is a fascinating agglomeration of various styles and eras. The oldest

Oriel window of the Old Town Hall (16th century) above the Gothic gateway to the courtyard.

The Old Town Hall dominates Hlavné námestie - the Main Square. To the left of its tower stands the Jesuit Church. The Gothic spire on the left belongs to the Franciscan Church.

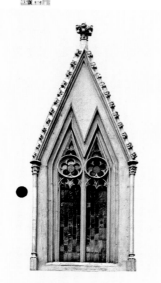

Cannon balls - like this one on the tower of the Old Town Hall - commemorate Napoleon's bombardment of 1809.

part is a fourteenth century house with a corner tower built for Mayor Jakob. In the fifteenth century the town bought the neighbouring house of Mayor Pawer and later had the Town Hall rebuilt and extended so as to match the importance of a free royal town. The original Gothic stepped gables on the Town Hall's houses were replaced in the sixteenth century by the long single-pitched roof visible today. In the same century the courtyard received a Renaissance arcade, the tower another storey and the neighbouring Ungerl house in the square was acquired. Following a devastating fire in 1733, the tower was

Courtyard of the Old Town Hall with Renaissance arcades from the sixteenth century. During the summer season, numerous concerts are held here.

In the 15th century a council room and a chapel were built on the first floor of the Town Hall.

restored in the Baroque style and another storey added, giving the tower its present look.

The east wing of the Old Town Hall with an eye-catching colourful roof dates from 1913.

In 1868 the Municipal Museum in Pressburg was founded, which has since occupied the first floor of the Town Hall. Little has changed since then, other than that its collections have got larger.

The new wings in Revivalist styles added in the early twentieth century and the ac-

A part of the museum's exhibition are the cellars, in the past used as the town's prison and torture chamber.

quisition of the Primate's Palace concluded the evolution of the Old Town Hall.

The dominant part of the Old Town Hall is an originally Gothic building with a tower dating from the 14th century. After a fire in 1733 the tower received its present Baroque appearance. For the best views of the Old Town and Castle visit the museum and climb the tower.

Its romantic atmosphere and the traditional Christmas market make Bratislava a popular destination in winter also.

THE PRIMATE'S PALACE ❹

The roof of the Primate's Palace is decorated with allegorical statues.

Designed by Melchior Hefele, this magnificent pink palace was built for Cardinal Joseph Bátthyány, Archbishop of Esztergom and Primate of Hungary. Completed within an incredible three years of construction in 1781, this building is one of the architectural jewels of Slovakia. Today it is part of the Bratislava City Hall.

It is documented that the site of the palace belonged to the Bishop from as early as 1370. With Esztergom having been captured by the Turks in 1543, the then Archbishop was forced to seek refuge in Pressburg and moved into the splendid Gothic residence of his predecessor, which at that time was the grandest building in the town. The palace saw much rebuilding throughout the centuries in order to accommodate a sovereign. By 1563 ses-

The elegant entrance of the largest palace in the Old Town - today a part of the Bratislava City Hall.

sions of the Hungarian Diet took place here and it was in that same year that Maximilian II was accommodated in the Archbishop's residence following his coronation as King of Hungary. At the end of the eighteenth century the older building no longer befitted the Archbishop's rank and was consequently replaced by the present grand palace.

Following the devastating fire in the Castle in 1811, the Hungarian kings occasionally stayed in the palace. Leopold II, however, was a guest in the palace as early as in 1790

Through a series of courtyards from the Primate's Palace one arrives in the Renaissance courtyard of the Ruttkay House from the 16th century.

The Archbishop's coat-of-arms on the Primate's Palace is topped by a Cardinal's hat.

following his coronation in St Martin's Cathedral. The palace's Hall of Mirrors, being suitable for important events, witnessed a coronation ball at the time when Ferdinand V was staying in the palace.

In 1805 the Primate's Palace became the venue for a historic event. On 26 December 1805, the Treaty of Pressburg was signed in the Hall of Mirrors, following the bloody Battle of Three Emperors at Austerlitz (today Slavkov in the Czech Republic). This treaty carved up large areas of Emperor Francis I's Austria and brought Napoleon to the peak of his power. To commemorate this glorious victory of the French, one of the streets leading to the Champs-Elysées in Paris was named "rue de Pressbourg". This peace treaty was signed by Prince von Lichtenstein on behalf of the Emperor of Austria and by

The two putti on the front façade hold the letters C and I representing the Archbishop's motto: "Clementia et Iustitia".

Open to visitors, the State Rooms of the Primate's Palace contain a unique set of English tapestries from the 17th century.

Foreign Secretary Talleyrand on behalf of Napoleon.

Several days prior to the Battle of Three Emperors, on their way to the battlefield, 10,000 French soldiers captured Pressburg. It was finally near Austerlitz (Slavkov) that they met the Austrian and Russian armies. Around 180,000 men met in a battle that ended after several hours and claimed 50,000 dead. In 1809 the French took up positions around Pressburg again; this time, however, the takeover was nowhere near as peaceful as in 1805. Some 18,000 soldiers on the right bank of the Danube under Marshal Davout besieged the town, which found itself under a heavy artillery bombardment for several

weeks. Despite withstanding the siege, Pressburg was eventually forced to surrender, following the decisive victory of the French at Wagram. The bombardment left large parts of

To commemorate the signing of the Treaty of Pressburg, a memorial plaque was inset in the wall of the Palace's foyer.

A must for every art lover: a set of six splendid tapestries, woven in Mortlake for Charles I.

the town damaged and to commemorate this sad event cannon balls have been preserved in the Old Town façades.

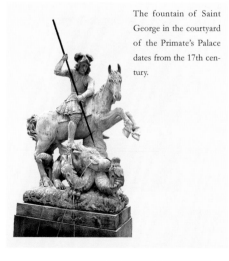

The fountain of Saint George in the courtyard of the Primate's Palace dates from the 17th century.

Open to visitors, the first floor of the Primate's Palace features magnificent State Rooms, the Hall of Mirrors where the Treaty of Pressburg was signed, and St Ladislas Chapel. The State Rooms contain the town's finest work of art - a set of six splendid English tapestries dating from the 17th century depicting the Greek legend of Hero and Leander. There remains a mystery, however, as to how they finished up in Pressburg from England.

The theory that they were woven for Charles I and later confiscated by Oliver Cromwell's Republicans and subsequently sold, seems probable. They are a product of the royal factory at Mortlake near London, established

View of the Primate's Palace. Coloured engraving, 19th century.

by James I by royal charter in 1619, who followed the example of a tapestry factory founded by the French King Henry IV. This particular set dates from 1630-32 at the time when the Mortlake factory was managed by Sir Francis Crane. The tapestries were woven from cartoons by Francis Cleyn by Flemish weavers under the famous master weaver Philip de Maecht, brought from Paris for this purpose. Rubens and Van Dyck were also among the artists that supplied cartoons. Following the town's purchase of the Palace from the Archbishop in 1903, restoration work was begun to adapt the building. It was a great sensation described by newspapers at home and abroad when the tapestries were discovered by chance after peeling off the wallpaper. When and why they were concealed has not yet been disclosed.

The tapestries were woven from a combination of silk and wool and, thanks to a long lasting organic dye and the fact that they were kept in darkness, they have preserved their original colours. Today the tapestries are a priceless work of art, as the Bratislava set remains the only complete set in the world with the markings of St George's Cross from Mortlake. Further incomplete sets and copies from Mortlake are to be found in Sweden and England.

GRASSALKOVICH PALACE ⑤

The eighteenth century saw noble families moving out of the crowded town within the town walls and building sumptuous residences in open spaces. Built in the 1760s in the Baroque style, the Grassalkovich Palace was designed for Count Anton Grassalkovich and is situated north of St Michael's Gate. Part of the whole complex is a French-style garden open to visitors. Being one of the most influential men in the country, Count Grassalkovich was President of the Royal Hungarian Chamber and became later advisor to Queen Maria Theresa. In the eighteenth century the Palace served as a

Presidential guard in front of the Grassalkovich Palace.

meeting place for the Hungarian aristocracy. One of the most important inventors of his time, Wolfgang von Kempelen, advisor to the Austrian court, a native of Pressburg, intro-

View of the Palace looking east. In the background the southern slopes of the Little Carpathians with vineyards starting on the edges of the city.

The restored Grassalkovich Garden is open to the public.

duced his new inventions, admired all over Europe - a chess machine that Napoleon is supposed to have played against in Vienna's Schönbrunn Palace, and a speaking machine - to high society in the Palace's elaborate State Rooms. The Palace witnessed a rich social life during the reign of Queen Maria Theresa, when elegant balls were frequently held here for the aristocracy. Being for decades the Kapellmeister of Prince Esterházy's court orchestra, Joseph Haydn was a guest in Pressburg on several occasions. One such was in 1772 when a ball to honour Duchess Maria Christine, Maria Theresa's favourite daughter, and Duke Albert von Sachsen-Teschen, Viceroy of Hungary, who resided in

Today the Grassalkovich Palace serves as the residence of the President.

Grassalkovich Palace at Christmas.

the Castle, was held in Grassalkovich Palace. Between 1897-1919 the Palace was the property of Duke Friedrich of Austria. Today the Palace serves as the residence of the President, while its Baroque garden remains open to visitors.

The presidential standard is made up of the Slovak coat-of-arms comprising a red field, three blue hills and a white double cross. When the standard is raised, the President is in the country.

The elegant interior of the palace is used for official audiences of the President.

WALKING TOUR

Most of Bratislava's sights and attractions are conveniently located within the Old Town and Castle Hill areas. The first part of this book concentrates on the historically most significant sights. The following pages will take you on a walking tour through the Old Town and its immediate surroundings with descriptions of additional important sights.

BRATISLAVA CASTLE ❶

History museum, Open daily 9.00-17.00 except Mon.,

Treasure Collection, Open daily 10.00-12.00, 13.30-16.00 except Mon., www.snm.sk

ST MARTIN'S CATHEDRAL ❷

Open Mon-Fri 10.00-11.45, 14.00-16.45, Sat 10.00-12.00, Sun 14.00-16.45

OLD TOWN HALL ❸

Municipal museum
Open daily 10.00-17.00, Sat-Sun 11.00-18.00 except Mon.

PRIMATE'S PALACE ❹

English tapestries, Hall of Mirrors.
Open daily 10.00-17.00 except Mon.

GRASSALKOVICH PALACE ❺

FRANCISCAN CHURCH ❻

The oldest church in the Old Town - Franciscan Church (13th century) - is located in the upper part of Františkánske námestie, adjacent to Hlavné námestie. This is where the newly crowned kings knighted selected noblemen as Knights of the Golden Spur. Attached to the north wall of the Franciscan Church is one of the jewels of Gothic art in Bratislava - the St John the Evangelist Chapel (14th century) - modelled after la Sainte Chapelle

in Paris. The Rococo Mirbach Palace opposite the Franciscan Church houses exhibitions of the MUNICIPAL GALLERY - sculpture and painting of the 18th and 19th century, temporary exhibitions. Open daily 10.00-17.00, except Mon.

ST MICHAEL'S GATE ❼

Michalská ulica (St Michael's street) leads to St Michael's Gate. The street's upper part is lined with Renaissance houses with cosy courtyards packed with little shops, galleries and wine cellars.

The tower of the gate contains the MUSEUM OF HISTORIC ARMS. Its balcony offers panoramic views of the Old Town and the Castle.
Open daily 9.30-16.30, except Mon.

BAŠTOVÁ ULICA ❽

Below St Michael's Gate is the narrowest lane in the Old Town - Baštová ulica - with several arches. In the past it was home to the town's hangman.

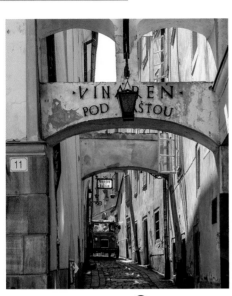

TRINITARIAN CHURCH ❾

Outside St Michael's Gate stands the Church of St John of Matha (Trinitarians). Finished in 1725, its interior is one of the finest examples of the Baroque in Bratislava. The grand trompe l'oeil fresco is the work of the Italian master Antonio Galli Bibiena.

Its original tall towers were probably destroyed during Napoleon's bombardment.

UNIVERSITAS ISTROPOLITANA ❿

The original edifice of the Universitas Istropolitana (founded in 1465), the first university within the territory of present-day Slovakia, in Ventúrska ulica. Today it is home to the Academy of the Performing Arts.

DE PAULI PALACE ⓫

The De Pauli Palace dating from 1770s in 1820

witnessed the first public concert of the then nine-year-old Franz Liszt.

ROYAL HUNGARIAN CHAMBER 12

The largest building in Michalská ulica is the University Library, originally the Royal Hungarian Chamber, built in 1756. In the 19th century sessions of the Hungarian Diet were held here.

PALFFY PALACE 13

The Palffy Palace – today the Austrian Embassy – was built in 1747 for Count Leopold Palffy, Marshall in the Austrian army. Its portal is one of the most beautiful of its kind in the town. In 1762 the six-year-old Mozart gave one of his first public concerts here for the local nobility.

KEGLEVICH PALACE 14

The Keglevich Palace was built in 1730 and was among the first Baroque palaces in town. Babette Keglevich, the Count's daughter, was one of the piano students of Ludwig van Beethoven, who gave a concert in the palace in 1796.

TOWN WALLS 15

Out of the town's originally extensive 15th century fortification, only its western part has been preserved. The remaining walls and three of the four town gates were demolished in the 18th century.

HOUSE OF THE GOOD SHEPHERD 16

This exceptional Rococo burgher's house from 1760s is so compact that it has only one small room on each floor. Today it houses the CLOCK MUSEUM displaying a collection of timepieces.
Open daily 10.00-17.00

CHURCH AND CONVENT OF THE POOR CLARES 17

This church dates back to the 14th century and serves today as a concert hall. The convent was rebuilt in the 17th century and in the 19th century housed a secondary school where the Hungarian composer Béla Bartók studied.

REDUTA 18

The sumptuous Reduta building (1913 - 19) contains the concert hall of the Slovak Philharmonic Orchestra. Between Reduta and the Danube, the Coronation Hill used to stand.

SLOVAK NATIONAL THEATRE 19

Designed by Viennese architects Fellner and Helmer (1884-1886), the Opera House of the Slovak National Theatre is a renowned stage attracting music lovers from home and abroad.

ČUMIL 20

The statue of Čumil conceived by artist Viktor Hulík is one of the favourite attractions within the

pedestrian zone.

THE MAIN SQUARE ㉑

In the Main Square different architectural styles meet. In the centre can be seen the town's oldest surviving fountain – the Maximilian Fountain dat-

ing from 1572. The eastern side of the square is dominated by the Old Town Hall, which consists of several interesting buildings. The opposite side of the square is occupied by one of the most beautiful Art-Nouveau buildings in town, designed by the well-known Budapest architect Edmund Lechner. The Kutscherfeld Palace on the north

side houses the French Embassy. Here, in 1847, lived and composed the Russian composer Anton G. Rubinstein.

JESUIT CHURCH ㉒

Built by the Lutherans in 1638, the church, by the king's decree, couldn't have a tower, or a presbytery or main entrance. Following an unsuccessful anti-Habsburg uprising, it was confiscated and given to the Jesuits. To commemorate the supression of the uprising, the king had a column of the Virgin Mary built in front of it.

HUMMEL'S HOUSE ㉓

The birthplace of the composer Johann Nepomuk Hummel is a tiny 17th century house hidden in a courtyard of a large turn-of-the-century building. Having studied with Mozart, Haydn and Salieri in Vienna, Hummel later succeded Haydn as kapellmeister with the Esterhazy family.

BLUE CHURCH ㉔

The Church of St Elisabeth (1909-13), designed in Art - Nouveau style, is one of the most beautiful churches in the city. It is usually referred to as the "Blue Church".

CHATAM SOFER MEMORIAL ㉕

In an underground mausoleum near the tunnel under the Castle Hill rest the remains of a Jewish cemetery used between 1670-1847 counting 23 graves and 41 tombstones. The most famous of all is the grave of Rabbi Chatam Sofer (1762-1839) who became one of the most significant Jewish scholars of his time.

MUSEUM OF JEWISH CULTURE ㉖

Housed in a 17th century building, the museum offers a complex view of the history, habits and

traditions of the Jewish community in Slovakia. Open daily 11.00-16.30 except Sat., www.snm.sk

LUTHERAN CHURCH 27

Finished in 1778, the city's largest Lutheran church replaced an older wooden structure. The then law did not permit Lutherans to build towers. It was used by the German community.

SLOVAK NATIONAL MUSEUM 28

The building of the museum was constructed in 1924 and today houses the Natural Sciences branch of the SNM. In front of the museum stands a memorial commemorating the founding of the first Czechoslovakia in 1918.

Open daily 9.00-17.00 except Mon., www.snm.sk

SLOVAK NATIONAL GALLERY 29

Being the largest and most important gallery in Slovakia, the SNG displays exhibitions ranging from Gothic to Contemporary art.

Open daily 10.00-18.00 except Mon., www.sng.sk

SNP BRIDGE 30

A modern landmark of Bratislava, the Nový most bridge was opened in 1971. Its two pylons are topped by a UFO - shaped panoramic restaurant with great views of the city and its surroundings.

FAMOUS COMPOSERS AND BRATISLAVA

JOHANN NEPOMUK HUMMEL

(1778-1837)

Born in Pressburg, Hummel went on to study with Mozart as a remarkable child prodigy. The predecessor of Liszt and successor of Haydn as Kapellmeister in the Esterházy household, he died as Kapellmeister at the Weimar court. Birthplace and museum in Klobučnícka ulica.

LUDWIG VAN BEETHOVEN

(1770-1827)

In 1796 Beethoven gave several concerts for noble families in Pressburg. He counted the Brunsvik and Keglevich families among his friends and among his admirers were young ladies from these families. Beethoven dedicated his Sonata for piano Opus 78 to Therese Brunsvik and gave piano lessons to Babette Keglevich. He probably also gave a concert in the Keglevich Palace in Panská ulica.

BÉLA BARTÓK

(1881-1945)

This famous Hungarian composer studied and lived for a part of his life in Pressburg.

WOLFGANG AMADEUS MOZART

(1756-1791)

As a six-year-old child prodigy, Mozart gave a concert in the Pálffy Palace for the local nobility.

JOSEPH HAYDN

(1732-1809)

As conductor of the court orchestra of Prince Esterházy, Haydn was a regular guest in the Esterházy Palace and his music was much in vogue. In 1772 he conducted a local orchestra in the Grassalkovich Palace at a ball to honour Duchess Maria Christine and Duke Albert von Sachsen-Teschen.

FRANZ LISZT

(1811-1886)

The career of the nine-year-old Liszt began in 1820 in the De Pauli Palace in Ventúska ulica, where he performed for the local nobility in his first public concert. He was a frequent guest in Pressburg and in 1884 he conducted his own Coronation Mass in St Martin's Cathedral.

WINE & BRATISLAVA

Wine-growing in Bratislava is as old as the city itself. The Celts, the Romans and later the Slavs grew vines on the slopes of the Little Carpathians around the present city. Vineyards were first referred to in the thirteenth century but following the invasion of the Mongol hordes in 1241 most of them were plundered. Thanks to the settlement of predominantly German-speaking craftsmen and vintners, wine-growing was revived. In 1435 there were already 474 wine-grower families living in the town, which meant that nearly all the inhabitants of Pressburg were in one way or another connected with the production of wine. It was first exported to Prague, later to what is now Austria and Germany. In 1579 most of the wine drunk in Prague was imported from the Little Carpathian region around Pressburg. Pressburg wine was a favourite with kings, too. King Matthias Corvinus (15th century) is supposed to have taken part in the grape harvest personally. The year 1825 saw the coronation of Caroline Auguste, consort of Emperor Francis I of Austria, in St Martin's Cathedral. On this occasion Napoleon II, son of Marie Louise of Austria and Napoleon Bonaparte, visited the town. After the coronation the whole royal family went to the vineyards and took part in the grape harvest. In the same year the company J.E. Hubert was established in Pressburg and became one of the first sparkling wine producers using the Champagne method outside France, its products being exported worldwide. The Hubert company has

A frequent evil in places with a surplus of wine, alcoholism is considered one of the weaknesses of the local people, too. When a group of like-minded people meet over wine, they are not able to end their tasting until they are intoxicated. When banqueting, they tend to go in for long and sometimes foolish toasts.

Matthias Bel 1736

been in production ever since. It is wines such as Riesling, Gewürztraminer, Silvaner, Pinot Gris and Grüner Veltliner known from Austria, Germany and the Alsace region in France that are typical of the region. The Old Town abounds in wine bars and cellars which are the best places to sample them.

BRATISLAVA'S SURROUNDINGS

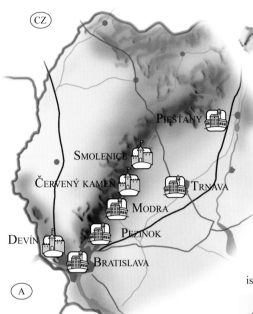

Castle has been a ruin ever since it was blown up by Napoleon's troops in 1809. The top platform offers breath-taking views of the neighbouring Lower Austria, Vienna and, on a clear day,s the peaks of the Alps. The hills overlooking Devín Castle are a paradise for hikers thanks to their rare fauna and well-marked nature trails with panoramic views.

PEZINOK AND MODRA

Located just 20 km northeast of Bratislava, Pezinok (population 22,000) is one of Slovakia's winemaking centres. The town

The Little Carpathians wine-growing region near Bratislava is noted, besides its wines, for ceramics production. The craft was introduced in the 16th century by immigrants from Italy and Switzerland. Today, mostly family-run businesses in the towns of Pezinok and Modra and their surroundings still make all their products by hand. The only larger company is the Majolika factory in Modra, where tours can be arranged.

DEVÍN CASTLE

Devín Castle, perched on a rocky outcrop above the confluence of the Danube and Morava rivers which constitute the border with Austria, is situated 13km to the west of the city centre. The

lies on the so-called Small Carpathians Wine Route, stretching some 60 km from Bratislava to Smolenice Castle. It connects all the important small towns and villages on the southern slopes of the Small Carpathians where winegrowing has been a

The massive Devín Castle towers above the Danube in the western part of the town.

The Town Hall with turrets and arcaded courtyard from around 1600 is one of Pezinok's most prominent buildings.

came to be stored there. Albrecht Dürer's designs were used to turn the castle into a perfect fortress which no one even attempted to conquer. In 1583, Mikuláš Pállfy, who became the castle's owner after marrying Mária Fugger, had the fortress remodelled as a prestigious residence. He invited many artists, predominantly from Italy. The Pállfy family, who remained the owners of the castle until 1945,

long-established tradition. In the centre, you will find typical wine-makers' houses with large drive-through gates and long courtyards. It goes without saying that each house has a wine cellar. The upper part of the town is dominated by a small chateau with a large English park, originally a water fortress built in the 13th century.

ČERVENÝ KAMEŇ CASTLE

Located in the Small Carpathians, not far from the wine town of Modra and some 30 km from Bratislava, Červený Kameň is one of Slovakia's best-preserved Renaissance castles. In the 13th century it was part of a chain of castles acting as a line of defence between the Hungarian and Bohemian kingdoms. In 1528 it became the property of the financier family of Fuggers from Augsburg. In a major reconstruction in the 16th century, vast cellars, 70-metres-long and 9-metres-deep were built, but they were never to be used for storing copper, as intended. Instead, it was wine, the typical product of the region, that

Throughout the year, the towns of Pezinok and Modra host a number of traditional festivals and events like e.g. the Exhibition of Wine in April, the Grape Harvest Festival in September, or the Days of Open Cellars in November. The cosy cellars of local wine producers are open to vintage lovers at any time of the year.

were keen travellers and collectors, who brought here many valuable items of furniture from all over Europe. The magical atmosphere and the amazing views from the castle are complemented by many other attractions, such as displays of birds of prey by the local falconers, and historical games.

SMOLENICE CASTLE

The original Gothic chateau was built in the 14th century at the foot of the Small Carpathians in western Slovakia to stand guard over a trade route to Bohemia. It changed hands many times over the centu-

ries, until it was acquired by the Pálffy family at the end of the 18th century. In the second half of the 19th century, an intricate romantic reconstruction was started, drawing on French and Italian medieval resources, and this continued into the 20th century. The complex of buildings is dominated by a massive central look-out tower with a beautiful view over the deep

Červený Kameň Castle, boasting the largest cellars in Central Europe, is one of the best-preserved castles in Slovakia.

forests of the Small Carpathians. The chateau is surrounded by a beautiful country park which gradually merges into the forest. A stroll around the area can be combined with a visit to the Driny Cave, the only one in the region. Nowadays the chateau, which can be found at the end of the 60-kilometre-long Small Carpathians Wine Route beginning in Bratislava, is used by the Slovak Academy of Sciences as a conference centre.

PIEŠŤANY

The most famous Slovak spa town, Piešťany (population 30,000) is situated on the river Váh, between the towns of Trnava and Trenčín. It is well-known for the healing properties of its hot springs, with a temperature of 67-69° C, as well as its healing mud, both of which rank among the world's best and most famous. Initially, spa guests bathed in holes in the ground filled with thermal water, and were provided with very basic accommodation in the houses of local residents. One of the people who underwent treatment in the spa in such primitive conditions was Ludwig van Beethoven in 1801. At the beginning of the 19th century, several spa buildings were constructed, known nowadays as Napoleon's Bathhouse, but the development was slow. Only in 1889 did a fundamental change take place,

The romantic Smolenice Chateau lies within beautiful natural surroundings.

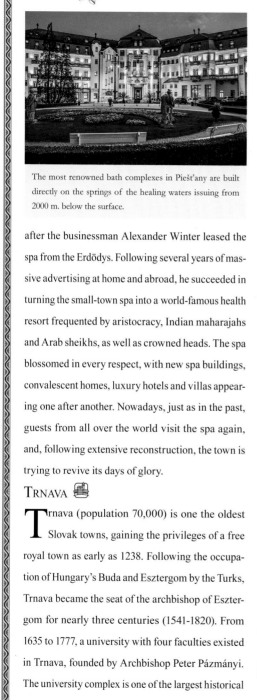

The most renowned bath complexes in Piešťany are built directly on the springs of the healing waters issuing from 2000 m. below the surface.

after the businessman Alexander Winter leased the spa from the Erdödys. Following several years of massive advertising at home and abroad, he succeeded in turning the small-town spa into a world-famous health resort frequented by aristocracy, Indian maharajahs and Arab sheikhs, as well as crowned heads. The spa blossomed in every respect, with new spa buildings, convalescent homes, luxury hotels and villas appearing one after another. Nowadays, just as in the past, guests from all over the world visit the spa again, and, following extensive reconstruction, the town is trying to revive its days of glory.

TRNAVA

Trnava (population 70,000) is one the oldest Slovak towns, gaining the privileges of a free royal town as early as 1238. Following the occupation of Hungary's Buda and Esztergom by the Turks, Trnava became the seat of the archbishop of Esztergom for nearly three centuries (1541-1820). From 1635 to 1777, a university with four faculties existed in Trnava, founded by Archbishop Peter Pázmányi. The university complex is one of the largest historical constructions in the town. It includes the first early-

Baroque building in Slovakia – the Jesuit church of St. John the Baptist (1629-1635), also called the University Church, designed by Antonio Canevale and built by Pietro Spazzo. The main square in Trnava is the Trinity Square, dominated by the Renaissance tower from 1574 and the Baroque Column of the Holy Trinity. Still standing in the nearby streets are attractive burgher houses of Gothic origin.

In 1846, Trnava was connected with Bratislava by the first horse-drawn railway in the then Hungarian Kingdom, which greatly helped its development. Nowadays, Trnava is once again a university town and one of the largest in the country, with a strong industrial base.

The finest burgher houses in Trnava are near the Renaissance tower dating from 1574.